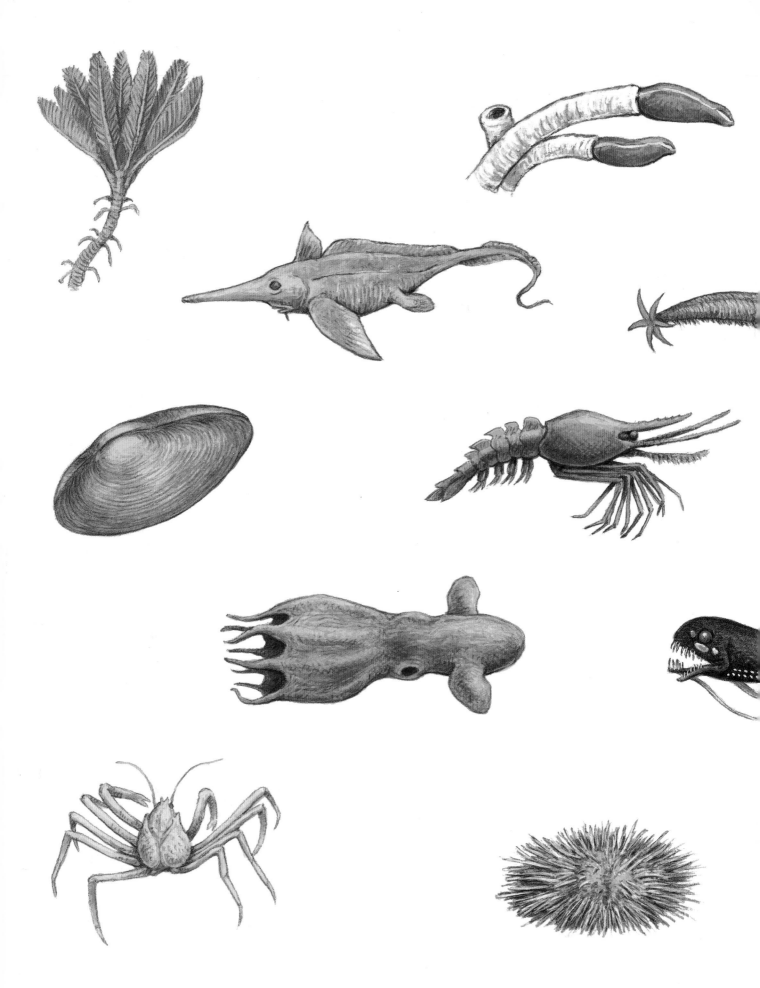

The Deep-Sea Floor

Sneed B. Collard III

Illustrated by Gregory Wenzel

 Charlesbridge

To Roger and Claudia, deep friends
and fellow explorers. With love—Sneed

To Karen—G. W.

Bold words are in the glossary on page 29.

Text copyright © 2003 by Sneed B. Collard III
Illustrations copyright © 2003 by Gregory Wenzel

Published by Charlesbridge
85 Main Street
Watertown, MA 02472
(617) 926-0329
www.charlesbridge.com

Library of Congress Cataloging-in-Publication Data

Collard, Sneed B.
  The Deep-sea floor / Sneed B. Collard III ; illustrated by Gregory Wenzel.
     p. cm.
Summary: Reveals the animal life that lives in the deepest oceans and
examines the technology that allows scientists to conduct research in
areas characterized by trenches, vents, and seeps.
  ISBN 1-57091-402-8 (jacketed reinforced) — ISBN 1-57091-403-6 (pbk.)
  1. Deep-sea animals — Juvenile literature. [1. Marine animals. 2.
Oceanography.] I. Wenzel, Gregory C., ill. II. Title.
  QL125.5 .C65 2003
  591.779—dc21   2002002281

Printed in South Korea
(hc) 10 9 8 7 6 5 4 3
(sc) 10 9 8 7 6 5 4 3 2

The illustrations in this book were done in watercolor
The display type was set in Adobe's Jimbo and the text type was set in Linotype's Sabon
Color separations were made by Sung In Printing, South Korea
Printed and bound by Sung In Printing, South Korea
Production supervision by Brian G. Walker
Designed by Susan M. Sherman and Gregory Wenzel

Far from land, a mile below the sea surface, a tripod **fish** rests on the bottom of the ocean. In total darkness, with water temperatures just above freezing, the fish silently waits for a meal. A shrimplike **copepod** (KO-peh-pod) drifts by. The tripod fish lunges and gulps it down, then settles back to wait for its next meal on the deep-sea floor.

Tripod fish swimming

Crinoids (KRY-noyds) sound like something from outer space, but they are really relatives of the sea star.

8

Cephalopods (SEH-fuh-luh-pods), whose members include octopuses and squid, live at many different depths. The *Vampyroteuthis* (vam-PIE-ro-tooth-is) is an unusual cephalopod, which is found between 700 meters (2,297 feet) and 4,000 meters (13,124 feet) below the surface.

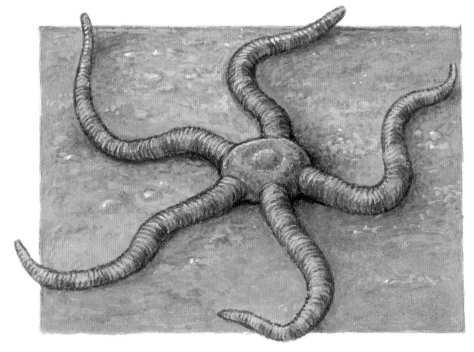

Brittle stars are among the many fascinating animals that make their homes on the deep-sea floor.

For most of history, the geography and animal life of the deep-sea floor have remained a total mystery. As recently as the mid-nineteenth century, many people believed that the ocean was bottomless or that no life existed in the deep. Others felt sure that the deep sea was filled with terrifying sea serpents or animals that had disappeared from shallower waters millions of years before.

In the 1870s, though, scientists began a serious search for deep-sea animals by lowering nets and other collection devices far below the surface. During World War I, they began mapping the ocean bottom with a new invention called **sonar**. The sonar made loud noises that bounced off the sea bottom. The echoes from these noises gave people a detailed outline of what the deep-sea floor looked like.

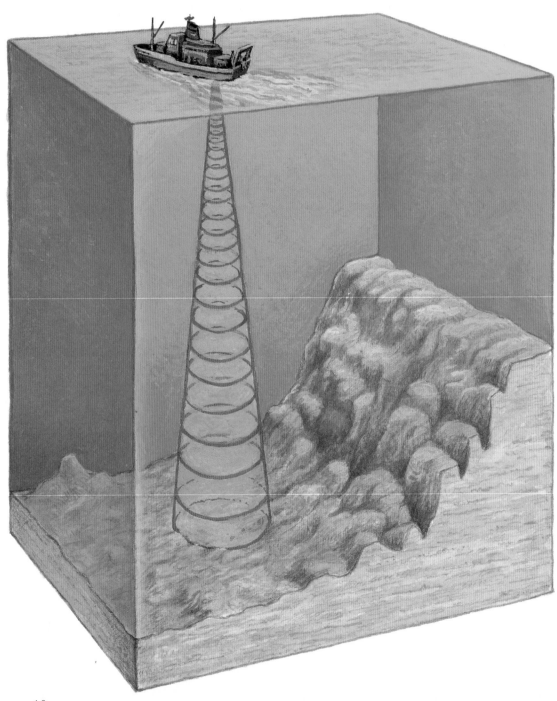

Epipelagic (eh-pee-pil-AH-jik) zone
0-200 meters (0-656 feet)

Mesopelagic (me-zo-pil-AH-jik) zone
200-1,000 meters
(656-3,281 feet)

1,000 meters (3,281 feet)

Bathypelagic (bah-
thee-pil-AH-jik) zone
1,000-4,000 meters
(3,281-13,124 feet)

2,000 meters (6,562 feet)

3,000 meters
(9,843 feet)

4,000 meters (13,124 feet)

Abyssopelagic (ah-biss-o-pil-AH-jik) zone
4,000-6,000 meters
(13,124-19,686 feet)

Like the land above sea level, the deep-sea floor rides around on huge **crustal plates.** In some regions, flat **abyssal plains** stretch for hundreds of miles across the tops of the crustal plates. In other places, the crustal plates collide or spread apart.

Where two plates collide, one plate may dive beneath the other, forming a **trench**. Trenches are the deepest places on our planet. The deepest known point on earth, the Challenger Deep, is in the Mariana Trench in the Pacific Ocean. The Challenger Deep is more than 11 kilometers (6.8 miles) deep. The Mariana Trench stretches 2,500 kilometers (1,554 miles) long and 70 kilometers (44 miles) wide along the deep-sea floor.

Where two plates spread apart, magma rises out of the earth to create huge underwater volcanoes and vast new mountain ranges or **ridges.** These mountain ranges run through every ocean on earth—more than 64,360 kilometers (40,000 miles) in all!

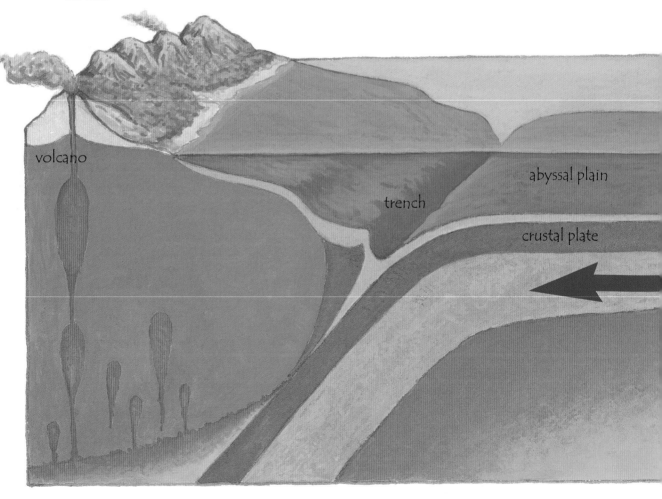

volcano

trench

abyssal plain

crustal plate

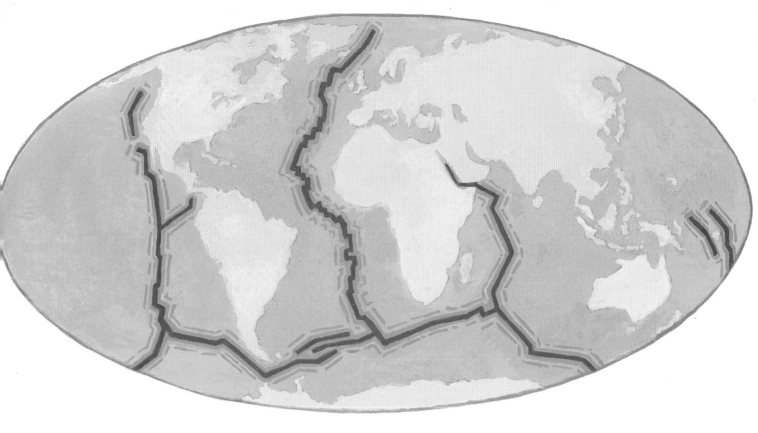

The earth's crust—including the ocean floor—is divided up into huge plates that slowly collide with and drift apart from each other, forming trenches and ridges.

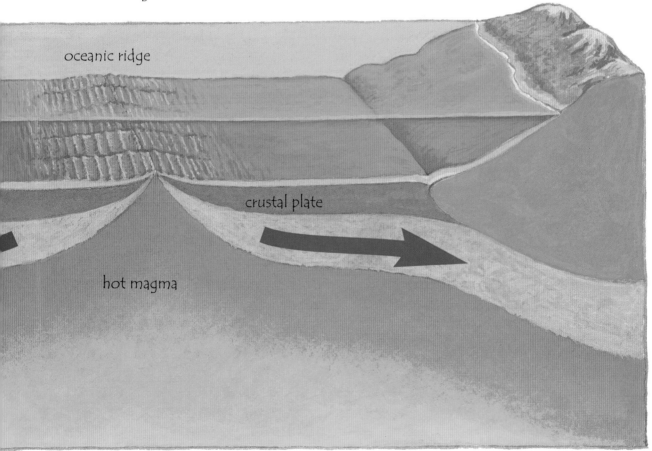

oceanic ridge

crustal plate

hot magma

From the abyssal plains to the deepest trenches, the deep-sea floor is a cold, dark place. At this depth, water pressure would crush a human, but amazingly, many animals thrive in this deep-sea world.

Shrimps, barnacles, worms, sea urchins, squat lobsters, sea squirts, sea spiders, and dozens of other kinds of animals make their homes in the depths. Most of these animals have more familiar relatives living in shallower water. But deep-sea animals live differently from their shallow-water relatives.

Galatheid (gal-ah-THEE-id) crab or
squat lobster

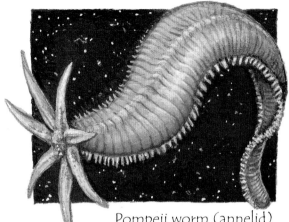

Pompeii worm (annelid)

Penaeid (peh-NA-id) shrimp

Spider crab

Deep-sea urchin

Deep-sea squid

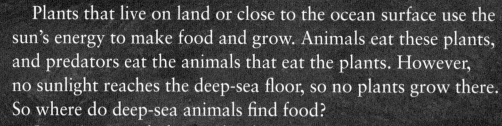

Plants that live on land or close to the ocean surface use the sun's energy to make food and grow. Animals eat these plants, and predators eat the animals that eat the plants. However, no sunlight reaches the deep-sea floor, so no plants grow there. So where do deep-sea animals find food?

Sometimes a whale or other large animal dies close to the ocean surface and sinks to the deep-sea bottom. This "whale fall" becomes a feast for scavengers, including fish, clams, crabs, and giant **amphipods** (AM-fih-pods) that can grow as long as eight inches. Some deep-sea animals also eat each other. But most deep-sea animals rely on two other sources of food—**fecal pellets** and **marine snow**.

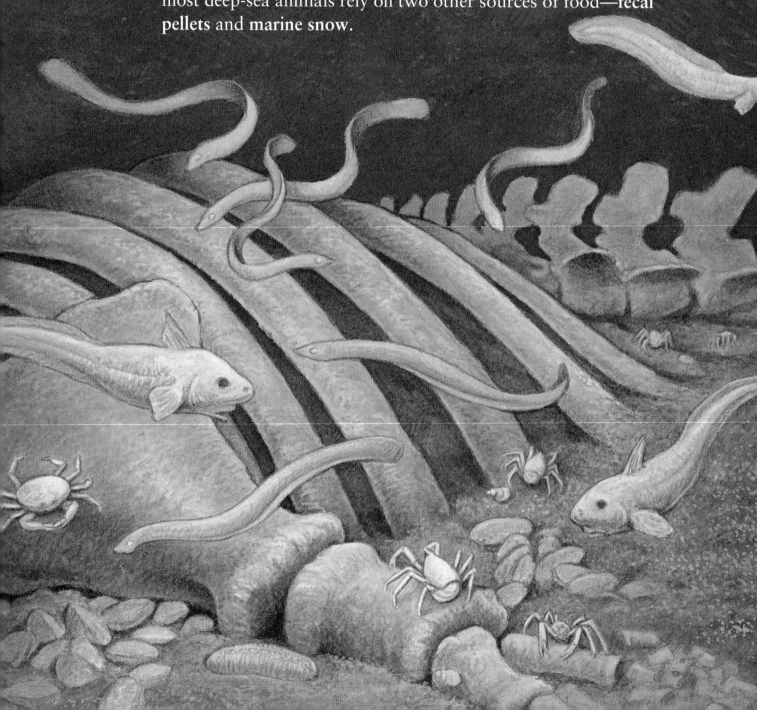

Sea cucumber and urchin

Fecal pellets are pooped out by many animals living in the ocean. Marine snow is made up of mucus, small pieces of dead plants and animals, and bacteria. Both fecal pellets and marine snow sink slowly down through the ocean depths to the sea floor. Scavengers such as worms, clams, and sea urchins pick up and eat these nutritious foods. Other deep-sea animals swallow **sediments,** digesting whatever morsels the sediments contain and pooping out the waste.

Deep-sea predators hunt the deep-sea scavengers. Sea anemones (ah-NEH-mah-nees), sea pens, and deep-sea corals—all relatives of jellyfish—capture copepods and other small creatures.

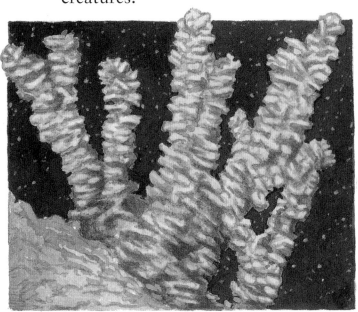

Coral

Sea pen

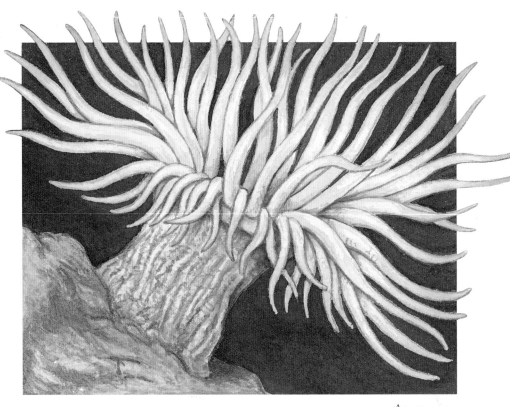

Anenome

One of the most beautiful groups of predators is the crinoids. Crinoids look like flowers, but they are actually relatives of sea stars. Many grow tall, delicate "stems." They filter the water in search of small animals and other tasty morsels that come along.

This pink creature isn't an umbrella. It's a cirrate (SEER-ate) octopus. Webs of skin and muscle connect the octopus's arms into a beautiful bell. The bell allows the octopus to swim like a jellyfish above the deep-sea bottom. It also helps the animal trap copepods—abundant, tiny shrimplike animals that are prey for many ocean animals.

Scientists have discovered more than 1,000 species of **fishes** living on or near the deep-sea bottom. Many have strange mouths and long, eel-like bodies. Rattail fishes swim with their heads slanted down. They stir up sediments and snap their jaws closed on any prey they uncover.

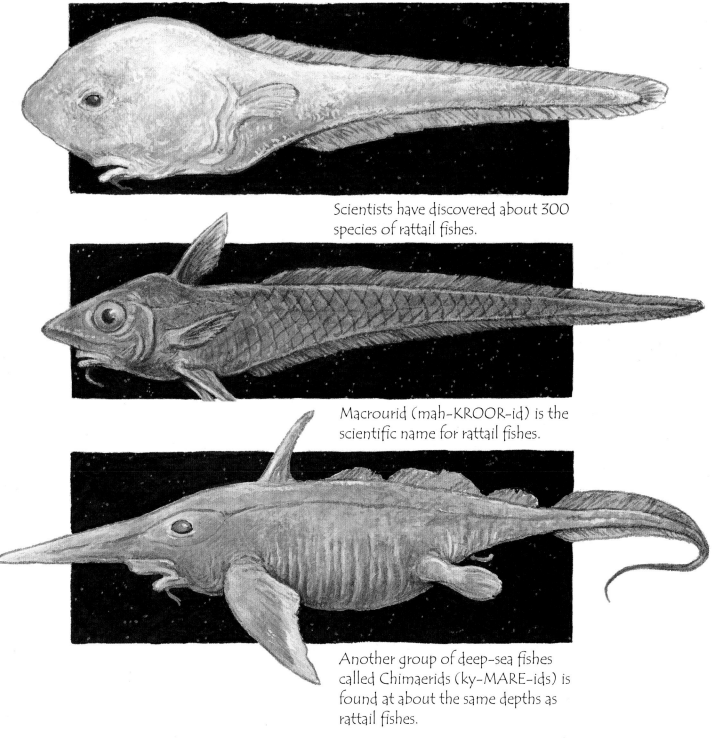

Scientists have discovered about 300 species of rattail fishes.

Macrourid (mah-KROOR-id) is the scientific name for rattail fishes.

Another group of deep-sea fishes called Chimaerids (ky-MARE-ids) is found at about the same depths as rattail fishes.

If you see a glow or flash of light along the dark ocean bottom at 1,000 meters (3,281 feet), you're not imagining things. Many animals here are **bioluminescent** (bi-o-loo-mih-NEH-sent)—they make their own light. Rattail fishes, for example, have light-producing bacteria living in little compartments on their undersides. These lights may trick predators into attacking the fishes' tails instead of their heads. Lights may also help different bioluminescent fishes identify each other and blend in with weak sunlight shining down from the surface.

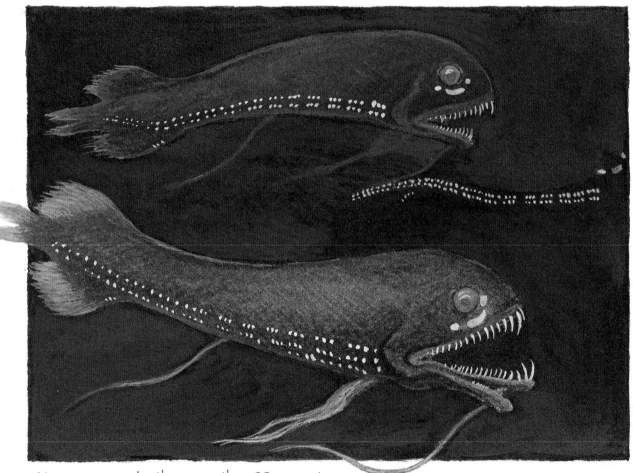

At some ocean depths, more than 90 percent of animals are bioluminescent, including the loosejaws.

Animals on the deep-sea floor aren't as abundant as land animals. That's because food is not as plentiful in the deep sea as it is on land. But in 1977, scientists aboard the research submersible *Alvin* discovered a startling concentration of animals.

The animals live at a **deep-sea vent**—a place where scalding hot water flows into the ocean from deep in the earth's crust. Here at the vent—more than 2,500 meters (8,200 feet) beneath the ocean surface—scientists found a thriving collection of mussels, crabs, limpets, giant clams, and giant tube worms called vestimentiferans (ves-tih-men-TIF-er-anz).

A deep-sea vent full of vestimentiferans. The black smokers in the back are chimneys built by minerals in the hot water pouring out of the sea floor.

At first, no one could figure out how these animals survived. Fecal pellets and marine snow couldn't possibly feed so many animals living in such a small area. But then scientists discovered remarkable kinds of bacteria living at the vents. These bacteria manufacture their own food from sulfides and other chemicals pouring out of the vents. Scientists call this process **chemosynthesis** (key-mo-SIN-theh-sis).

Some vent animals, such as limpets and shrimp, graze on the bacteria directly—and become food for predators living around the vents. Other vent animals, such as the vestimentiferans, have bacteria growing inside their bodies. The bacteria make and release food that feeds the worms. Scientists have discovered chemosynthetic bacteria in other places besides deep-sea vents.

Crabs and tube worms are just some of the animals that make their living at deep-sea vents.

Cold seeps—where energy-rich chemicals pour out of the sea floor from underlying sediments and rock layers—also support remarkable animals found nowhere else on earth.

Before these discoveries, scientists believed that almost all life relied on **photosynthesis** (fo-toh-SIN-theh-sis)—the ability of plants to make food from the sun's energy. Now scientists realize that there are at least two systems of life on earth—photosynthesis and chemosynthesis. Some people even believe that life on earth may have started with chemosynthesis at places such as vents and seeps. If so, perhaps life could have evolved on other planets in the same way.

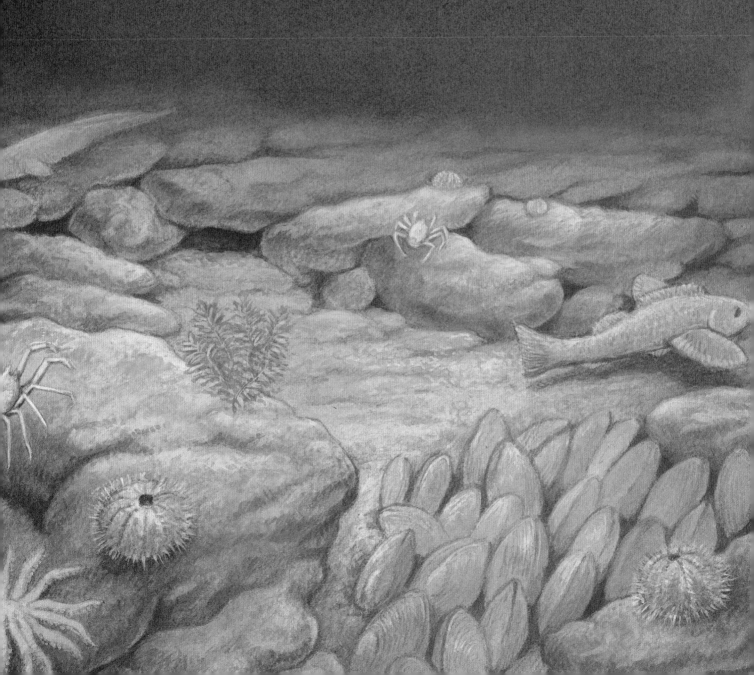

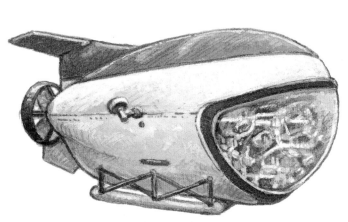

Russia's *Mir* can dive to
6,090 meters (19,980 feet).

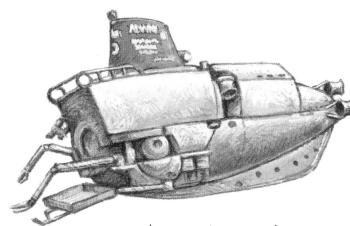

The United States' *Alvin*
can dive to 4,500 meters
(14,764 feet).

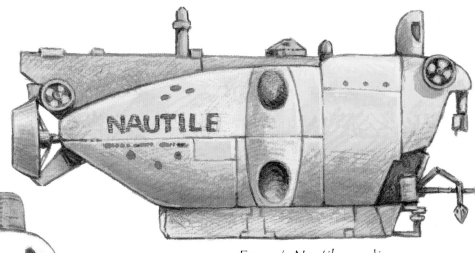

France's *Nautile* can dive
to 6,000 meters
(19,685 feet).

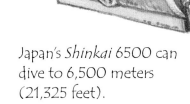

Japan's *Shinkai* 6500 can
dive to 6,500 meters
(21,325 feet).

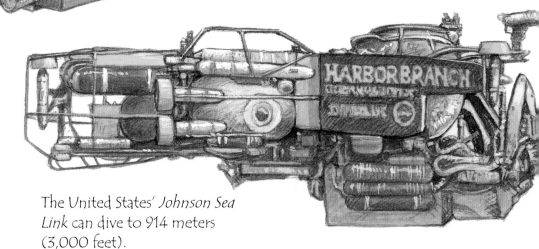

The United States' *Johnson Sea
Link* can dive to 914 meters
(3,000 feet).

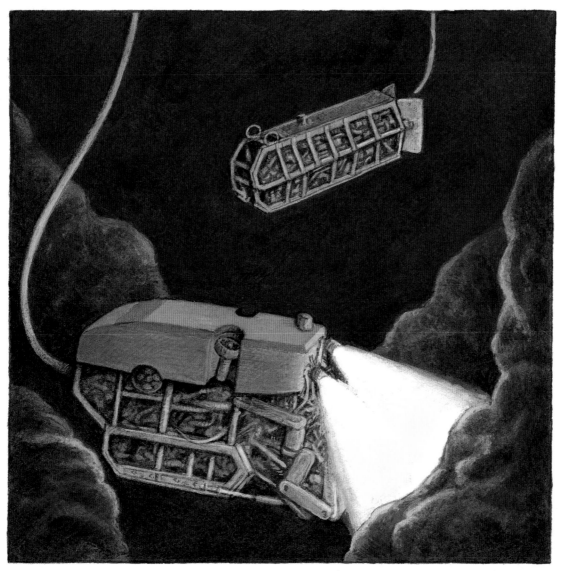

The United States' Jason (bottom) and Argo systems are unmanned remote-controlled vehicles.

Scientists continue to explore the deep-sea floor using better and better equipment. Deep-sea submersibles carry scientists directly into the depths. Unmanned remote-controlled vehicles also explore the deep sea. The vehicles allow scientists to study the chemistry, geology, geochemistry, and biology of the deep sea. Scientists can observe and investigate, for example, how deep-sea animals spread from place to place and how vent animals deal with poisonous chemicals and acidic waters pouring out of the vents.

As humans explore the deep-sea floor, we will continue to make fascinating discoveries. One thing we have already learned is that the deep sea needs protection. Pipelines, dredges, and fish trawls have already damaged many areas of the deep-sea floor. Mining on the ocean floor also has the potential to destroy the homes of many deep-sea animals. Our challenge will be to explore and use the deep sea while keeping it healthy for future generations.

Glossary

amphipods A group of crustaceans whose bodies have many segments. They look similar to the common pill bugs found in gardens.

abyssal plains Large regions of the deep-sea floor that are almost absolutely flat.

bioluminescent A word describing animals, plants, and other living organisms that make their own light.

chemosynthesis The process of making food by splitting chemical bonds to produce energy.

cold seeps Places where cold, chemical-rich waters pour out of the sea floor.

copepod An abundant, tiny shrimplike animal that is prey for many ocean animals.

crustal plates Large plates upon which the earth's continents and sea floors reside and drift.

deep-sea vent A place where superheated water full of energy-rich chemicals pours out of the deep-sea floor.

fecal pellets Poop from animals; they are a food source for many marine animals.

fish A cold-blooded aquatic animal, usually having fins and gills. Term refers to a single fish or more than one fish of the same or different species.

fishes Term refers to more than one species of fish.

marine snow Pieces of mucus, body parts, and dead animals that sink down through the ocean, forming a food source for many deeper-living animals.

photosynthesis The production of food using light energy from the sun.

ridges Volcano and mountain ranges arising in places where two crustal plates are pulling away from each other, allowing magma to rise from deep in the earth.

sediments Soil or other material that settles to the bottom of a liquid, such as water.

sonar A device that records the location of the sea floor and other underwater objects by making loud pinging noises and recording the echoes of the pings as they bounce off the objects.

trench A deep submarine canyon formed where one of the earth's crustal plates is diving beneath another.

To Find Out More . . .

Books

Widder, Edith. *The Bioluminescence Coloring Book*. Fort Pierce: Harbor Branch Oceanographic Institute, 1998.

Connor, Judith, & Bruce Robison. *The Deep Sea*. Monterey, CA: Monterey Bay Aquarium, 1999.

Earles, Sylvia. *Dive: My Adventures in the Deep Frontier*. Washington, D.C.: National Geographic Society, 1999.

Collard, Sneed B. III. *Our Wet World: Exploring Earth's Aquatic Ecosystems*. Watertown, MA: Charlesbridge, 1998.

Web Sites

www.hboi.org The Harbor Oceanographic Institution, which operates the *Johnson Sea Link* deep-sea submersibles, has a great bioluminescence section on this Web site.

www.divediscover.whoi.edu This interactive Web site of the Woods Hole Oceanographic Institute features deep-sea expeditions by *Alvin*.

www.mbayaq.org The Monterey Bay Aquarium site shows deep-sea explorations into Monterey Canyon.

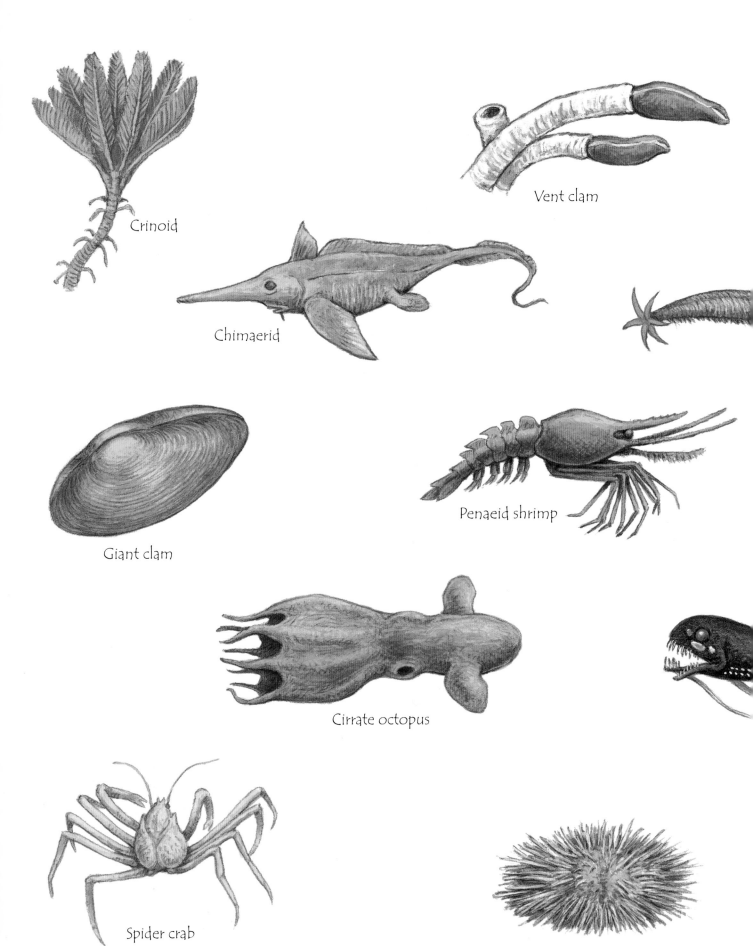

Crinoid

Vent clam

Chimaerid

Giant clam

Penaeid shrimp

Cirrate octopus

Spider crab

Deep-sea urchin

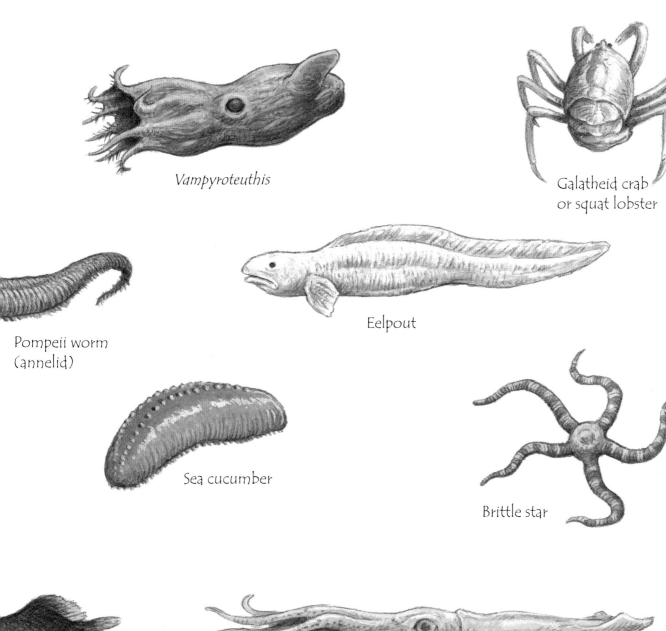

Vampyroteuthis

Galatheid crab
or squat lobster

Pompeii worm
(annelid)

Eelpout

Sea cucumber

Brittle star

Loosejaws

Deep-sea squid

Vent crab

Anenome